Zinc Fingers

PITT POETRY SERIES

Ed Ochester, Editor

Zinc Fingers

Poems A to Z

Peter Meinke

University of Pittsburgh Press

Published by the University of Pittsburgh Press, Pittsburgh, Pa., 15261
Manufactured in the United States of America
Printed on acid-free paper
10 9 8 7 6 5 4 3 2 1

Cover art: *Circe*, a lithograph by Eugene Larkin, 1964

The publication of this book is supported by a grant from the Pennsylvania Council on the Arts

for Gretchen,
who told us about Zinc Fingers

Contents

O to Z

On the Arrangement of These Poems

The title poem, "Zinc Fingers," suggested to me an alphabetical arrangement, and when I looked through my poems, I saw I had at least one poem for each letter (counting "The Examiner's Death" for "X"). This arrangement isn't a new idea, of course—Ashbery and Auden have done it, to remember alphabetically—but I like the accidental associations, older poems with newer poems, villanelles with free verse, dark with light, "The Brain" between "Assisted Living" and "Certitude," and I hope the reader enjoys them this way, as well.

Absence

Some people like broken glass
are known by absence:
she's one of those students
who never go to class

like unpublished scribblers
known for what
they might have done if not
for the job and the little nibblers

unvoiced echoes
of an agonized shout
someone thinks about
shouting but never does

as with a childless marriage
a couple's bind
is negatively defined
like a horseless carriage

as with an air of distraction
twiddling the doorknob
the man from Porlock
made a great subtraction

One can get further away
from life than one might imagine
like a would-be has-been
not catching on in papier mâché

or a man (say) working in rhyme
his insides much
out of touch
with the times

Apples

. . . the apple I see and the apple
I think I see and the apple
I say I see
are at least three
different apples . . .
    One sympathizes with Dr. Johnson here
when he kicked a stone
to refute the Bishop: such
airy-fairy distinctions   so much
applesauce!

    And yet when you say
what I think you say
in a way that may
or may not be final I can only hope
that cold stone that white boulder that
    . . . iceberg between us
is not really there but sliding
like some titanic idea
through the North Pole
in the apple of my eye . . .

Arthritis in St. Petersburg

Heat in August flattens everyone
brittles the potted ferns in three quick
days if you forget to water
Sun hammers the road and you
drive toward a slick
shimmer always a dream away
elbowskin flapping
like a lizard's neck

But is that you really?   It's others
who grow old although this octogenarian
paradise declines like sour milk like bread
with its webbed mold or ruined apples
and pears that scare you twice: once
when you see the hole and once when the roach runs up
     your arm:
these diluvial creatures
can only mean you harm

The older you are the harder to cope:
on fixed incomes scattered scarecrows
haunt the waterfront
mope around the park in second-
hand clothes wondering what hit them:
Nobody knows!   The newspaper claims
the deficit is huge   The oil
embargo jacks the price of rouge

And even you against your will
find you talk more and more about
your health: the proper diet
price of vitamin pills the warped
apportioning of your country's wealth
the way the summer makes your fingers swell
while the young artists in Banana Republic shorts
plan their next show at the Vinoy Beach Resort

Assisted Living

Hunching at the adult center
like aluminum crickets
on the ground-floor hallway
outside the arthritic elevator
our chrome appendages clanking
and hooking each other we stuff
ourselves in the box and turn around

Language is queer: adult movies
mean fucking but adult centers
mean dying though both mean
without dignity in front of others
In the elevator our spotted hands
and heads shake like mushrooms in rain

Not one in here who hasn't had
adventure   We've cried out
in bed and staggered home at midnight
sung songs and lied made
hellish mistakes and paid for them

or not: it makes small difference   Life
is gravity dragging all together:
the sparkiest eye the delicate breast
the sly hand the harsh laugh . . .

If there were humor left in this small band
it would raise its drying voice and shout
knowing most are deaf: *Going down!*

But no one says a word so we wait
nodding fungily for someone

to press our number

The Brain

Sometimes I have to shake my brain
like a bad child: *Behave you little shit*
Politically incorrect
pimpled cerebrum a real pain

it must hate authority:
when a Great Man speaks
it squeaks
It needs a shot of WD-40

When a Wise Woman talks
for my soul's health
and I need to listen well:
Nice bottom! it squawks

In any serious place
halls where they knot their ties
I tend to cross my eyes:
my brain's unlaced

yet just as I'm about to shoot it
through my left ear
it murmurs from God knows where:
The hard rain goose-steps

forward and the crooked grasses
of our meadow whisper like lawyers:
it's unfair and mysterious
but my murderous mood passes

and I decide to keep this clown
Seems worth it on the whole
with a little damage control:
trying to hold it down

when it's around mature people
Won't you *ever* grow up? I beg
It answers   like a dog lifting its leg
Does the Pope pee purple?

Certitude

Tomorrow if it come

I (if I'm around)
will barricade our home
from the hullabalooing town
corking the walls of my room

unless I decide to go out
walking the clanking streets
in the marvelous city noise

savoring all that din
unless I decide to pop in
for a quiet drink with the boys . . .

I suffer gladly
this foolish uncertainty
for which we've found no cure
I'm confused therefore I'm alive:

still lie the dead sure

Circce

for Eugene Larkin

Well her eyes were slanted slow and brown
and large enough to let us see the whites
before we slammed the shore   We slept each night
outside her door and listened to them bound
from bed to floor   Her breasts were small and tight
shoulders round   Her thighs (we all could see) were white:
in short her attributes were fine
and we turned tipsily into swine

I tell you Ulysses saved us no doubt
after he had his fill and wanted out
but as for me to see that lady strut her stuff
I'd grunt and snortle in the trough
A man turned pig by a goddess can't be blamed:
in front of power like that why should I feel ashamed?

The Cliff at Gorge de l'Areuse

When Tim was a little boy he slipped
and slid down a mountain and was saved
at the final instant from flying
over a cliff into a river
bed a hundred yards below   This is
a source of humor now but we all
shook for days and still shake in our dreams
dreams our in shake still and days for shook

No one told us fear is half of love
love of half is fear us told one no
and travels with your heart like the black
box that's always on the plane beneath
the glowing dials indestructible
as the longing for poetry and
meaning so when we die angelic
scientists can diagnose our lives

sifting through tears and scars of nightmares
nightmares of scars and tears through sifting
printed deep as twelve-point Monaco:
'scarlet fever' 'car crash on Boonton
Road' 'retinitis pigmentosa'
High among these brooding images
they'll find 'Gorge de l'Areuse' the leaves wet
that day the long slide the saving hand . . .

They say that words are arbitrary
building blocks constructing sentences
meaningless and unreliable
but roll them as you will reverse sub-
divide them into pure syllables
of sound when we say 'Tim' or 'cliff' the
love and fear we feel tastes real as air
air as real tastes feel we fear and love

Coal

To think
this semibituminous lump blackening
my fingers was once stem petal and leaf
brash red and luminous yellow
green tendril of vine
hugging stubborn stumps
lingering in swamps dying beyond grief
Pressure and time squeezed
color and warmth century-slow
into this hard black ball of a
coal

but they're still in there:
they flare out and escape
when place person and heat are right

Tonight
I think of the pressure of time
as the coal flames green and red
and yellow in our flickering room   I think
with you I feel immortal for a moment
and the bright colors of your hair
and dress are elements that seem
permanent white breast and arm
proof against that blackening
roof closing in like God's geologic
glove

Coffee

coffee in airplanes
poured by girls with pressurized faces
kicks off dreams that range
beyond the land's desires
absolute dreams
corrupting absolutely
kicking over the traces
of gravity envisioning strange
couplings with godlike birds
unbanking the fires of pain
and madness muted by will
and habit and morning coffee

Morning coffee braces the rational,
lines up agendas, committees,
and classes; untangles the
wires that pull us like puppets
through another stage of another day.

but coffee in airplanes
tricks us by seeming the same
and as soon as we sip it
we find we are lifted away
above guidelines and charts we
are out of our minds
with fierceness and joy of freedom
that carry us to an oasis
of untrammeled self-indulgence
in passions and ashes of passions
till the No Smoking sign flashes on
and we businesslike get down to cases

Driving through a Storm near Boothbay Harbor

She wants to pull over and stop but he
grows stubborn and noses into waves
of water drubbing the car like buckets
poured from a parapet to repel invaders

No lights glow on this road and when
a speeding truck soaks them in its wake
she knows all over America men
are driving out of control and she

a captive historical statistic

stares at nothing with small white fists
and a heart whacking back&forth because
he's showing her he fears neither
lightning nor the fingers of floodtide

grabbing the treadless tires so the car
lurches drunken and profane on this
their second honeymoon while she starts
to cry and memories rise through the night

like dark islands off the coast of Maine

Each Morning

I get up a drag
soft teeth fat tongue flatulent & flab
crawl to the bathroom heavy as a cow
hand lurches to the jar on the 2nd shelf
gnarls it out & pops my yellow bomber

O yellow bomber golly wow

Pantothenic acid charges my blood cells
hacking down the histamines
niacin flushes my cheeks watch out world
riboflavin teams with hydrochloric acid
no anemia today boys
the others pitch together each does his part

to get me out of there with a hopped-up heart

But the last ingredient
microscin
does no good at all
just hangs around my system
because it likes me

Election

I know this is crazy
but I think I'm losing my mind

On the other hand
if I *were* crazy
I wouldn't think I'm losing my mind
so I must be sane

but that's what all crazy people think

Let's get hold of this
I am either
(a) crazy
or (b) sane:
if I am (a)
I wouldn't know if I were crazy *or* sane

because I'd be crazy

However
if I am (b)
I would *know* I was sane

unless I were crazy

To sum up: it seems
I'm in no position to judge these things
and it's up to you the reader
to decide the question
Unfortunately you know nothing about it
Nevertheless
that's the way we work
so I'd be happy to have a vote
and get this thing off my back

Finches on Aycock Street

I used to throw a scuffed baseball for hours
hours & hours!   gripping it hard along
the seams for curves flipping my wrist inside out
to get the screwball fading across the plate:
Time well spent because today hearing the girls
and boys of Greensboro play in early spring
despite the palsied tulips the thin bare trees
stark as fish spines in the chill the exact same

happiness returns

with the sounds the smack in glove their high cries: *Pop*
it in there! No hitter up there   no hitter!
And though because I bend above this desk all
day producing nothing much our neighbors think
Poor sonofabitch when the cries of baseball
from across the street slide into the branches
of my brain every base is a bag of gold
like those finches on the dark limbs of our mag-

nolia: *Look! We're rich!*

Fortunato Pietro

Learning a new language is like
falling in love again   That's why
the young are better at it: they
enter the field of the past
participle with no fear
of the tongue's betrayal

O my new love I am sorry
I stammer and falter
that I cannot always rise
al occasione   But as I graze
among your suffixes
and prefixes your liquid

vocabolario and feminine
endings though my knees buckle
and my verbs freeze
my heart declines
to learn on its own: *O bella*
molto bella bellissima!

Francis

When my heart heaves like a hooked
fish and breath creaks crooked as hairpins
from my lungs I remember Francis our sweet-
tempered cat who poisoned by Christian neighbors
limped into the garden breathing hard
curled in camellia shade and died   modest
and self-effacing as a fern closing
his delicate ears to the mockingbird's laugh

Francis believed in heaven purring in paradise
fourteen years plying his roles as killer
and comforter guiding our children
through catnip grace the double-hinged
doors of conflicting claims
death and the rights of mice

Grandfather at the Pool

Now that I'm old
respectable and white and pink
you tease like bold
hotblooded courtesans who think
old men prefer thin beer to drink

But I could take
the whiskey of your lips and eyes
and still not slake
this thirst for brandy-colored thighs:
this the dead end of growing wise

The bubble in
our blood will boil and sing: the heart
has never been
a dry bright and studious part
but in dark chambers plies its art

So let it be
that youngsters at this sunny pool
have sport with me
and set me dancing like a fool:
we have millenniums to cool

A Handheld Camera Visits Billy's Bar
at Happy Hour

Set-up shot across the street
focusing on blinking signs
selling cut-rate beer & wine:
HAPPY HOUR! DOUBLE TREAT!!

Buildings in the neighborhood
hunch as if to ward off blows
Bricks crack like pistachios
termites tumble through the wood

Gin and vodka like a pair
of hookers on the sticky bar
call us in to park the car
by the peeling doorway there

Maraschino cherrystems
curl upon the table top
near a leaky coffee cup
crumpled napkin slick with phlegm

Soggy coasters advertise
everything the heart desires:
instant banking of the fires
constant blanking of the eyes

Jesus Mavis help me out
Voices fight the tv screen
showing some athletic team
showing us what life's about

If there only were an inch
of passion or fidelity
in this hole where Ladies pee
like broken horses on a ranch

and Gentlemen swell prostates by
squatting paralyzed for hours
nursing beers and whisky sours
spotting on their shirts and flies

and all of us forget the words
to songs and hymns our parents knew
God of our Fathers stuck like glue
in the beaks of dodo birds:

then the camera might sweep
piously across our way
catching us about to pray:
Do re mi fa so la ti

A Hawk in Athens

In that summer of boats and châteaux
a hawk dipped below us and turned
in his search for delicate mice
and looked us hard in the eye

In that summer of boats and châteaux
we struck an immovable rock
so the captain was flipped in the air
like a mouse with a hawk on his neck

In that summer of boats and châteaux
the Acropolis shimmered and burned
while I scampered from rampart to rampart
unclasping and clasping your hand

In that summer of boats and châteaux
the mountains were mounded like breasts
and we sailed in the day and the dark
till we caught on a fisherman's net

In that summer of boats and châteaux
we slept in a canopied bed
The windows were deep as our arms
the drapes an unsettling red

In that summer of boats and châteaux
in a park by the harbor at Morges
we lay in the shadow of trees
whose leaves were as pointed as swords

In that summer of boats and châteaux
you leaped from the table and cried
and the years have fled by ever since
like mice trying vainly to hide

History

. . . everything going back so far the main
thing the thing that determines how
you think and feel is where and when you got
your ticket   The ball spins on a turtle's back
at 66000 miles per hour and suddenly
you're in: a Ukrainian milkmaid Republican
blueblood preregistered at Yale a terrorist
chewing woodsticks in a tin shack . . .

. . . hard to take credit or blame:
the world would have been different
if Charlemagne had been taller if Hitler
had been told he had talent if Stalin
had felt secure   You reading this poem
think what you might have become
if your mother hadn't died your father
didn't drink your nose had been smaller . . .

. . . and they died and drank because X
happened and Y didn't   Circumstance
like an elephant's foot squashes us
among the peanut shells   We grab our
assigned seats and hang on   Tumbling juggling
the high wire are out of the question for most
of us in town for the show: We're the house!
Count us as we shout *Bring on the clowns!* . . .

Home on Cape Cod

We've seen colossal sights together dazzling
to the heart: the rusty ruins of Petra
eroding in the Dead Sea winds dark alleys
twisted through Luxor the Nile the Rhinefalls Etna
in its bright burning the brutal calendar
of Stonehenge the Great Wall where we cried
out loud overwhelmed by fright or wonder:
and the Gorge where Timothy slipped and nearly died

Still of all those visions that enthralled my eyes
the one repeating daily like a muezzin's call
is that of you by our window in a dressing gown
brushing your matchless hair and saying with a sigh
perhaps I *had* made you happy after all:
I and the little roses of Provincetown

A Hot Day in June

I

am stuck in my car on
a hot day in June and
in front of me the wat
er recedes at 50 miles
per hour always 100 y
ards ahead shimmering
in the summer sun: a m
irage of course it's not t
here at all and yet in th
is nothing that doesn't e
xist there are reflections
of trees and cars and tel
ephone poles perfectly c
lear though inverted: so
clear that if I could only
get closer I think I could s
ee the black eyes of that r
ed-shouldered hawk I cou
ld find the lines of poems s
hining there in this mirror
of sky that lies before me l
ike a gift I have been reach
ing for all my life holding t
hat beautiful real bird accor
ding to some miraculous law
of the mind's bright distorting

eye

The House on Taylor Avenue

We have photographs if you need to see some proof:
a gray house with bay windows pitched roof
and a soaring purple lilac in the yard
A soccer practice field for women now: hard
to imagine anything else ever there
but instead of players' cries we strain to hear
our children's voices high as birdsong
in larky protest from the darkening lawn

A little longer! Please! Just one more game!
We'd groan theatrically rolling their names
like mantras through the thickening filigree
of dusk: *Perrie Peter Gretchen Timothy* . . .
And of course they've all flown now every one
grown and gone off to their own concerns
while we stand here on Taylor Avenue
staring at emptiness like a scenic view

They say everyone loses everything
at the end so this is just foreshadowing:
health houses children dignity shot to hell
like some late payment due for living well
But as our house still echoes in our heads
so we in the world's although the world be deaf:
trembling strings restored and newly strung
reverberating in an unknown tongue

like some fixed piece of music whose notes
are printed on our nuclei and float
in indestructible particles toward birth
as we disintegrate in flames or earth
explaining someone else's *déja vu*
in Delhi Paris London or Montreux:
a vision with children opening like flowers
when some dreaming stranger turns upon our house

The Housekeeper in London

Mrs B had small eyes hard and quick
as crows: you could never catch them

looking at you   They'd flit around the room
from limb to limb as if a bat were banging

blind above us   'Them students live like pigs'
she spat at me   'the filth under their beds'

Her husband was alcoholic   her boy
a plumber's helper   She weighed thirteen

stone   Just then our most slender student
stopped by   asking for a key (she had lost her own)

Mrs B's   mouth smiled   'Here you are   then   luv'
We watched the student sway along the hall

inherited blood singing in her ankles
Branches heaved everywhere: the crows

landed and Mrs B looked me in the eye
for the first time: 'Rich bitch'   she said

The Humane Trap

The rat's picked dry & clean as ash
in the humane trap I forgot
left all winter in the garage
By the time we returned his flesh

was gone skeleton
polished by roaches ants
He was done with his rodent dance
(or *she* now cold unsexed as stone)

who chewed holes through our birdseed sacks
& after that our windowsill
and flowerbox & luggage till
we declared war and set the traps

So now I stare at the abstract shape
in its wire prison fetally curled
glowing bright as mother-of-pearl
with perfect teeth agape

then place her bones light as meringue
on a plate that holds curved and frail
ribs like eyelashes saurian tail
next to our bed from which it sings

some stygian rat song in a voice
both male and female O *why should a dog a horse
have life* it sings and I of course
knowing it really doesn't just close my eyes . . .

but still against my pillow I can hear
like steps on snow on its forced march
to the last gulag through a crumbling arch
my heartbeat crunching in my ear

and though we slog together mile on mile
and pick up speed as we approach the end
we can't shake the shadow of this new friend
his little skull her little rabid smile

Ibises

Nothing so parsed as a Florida
morning after a night rain: like pale
semi-colons lines of hunched ibises
punctuate our lawns   On her dawn walk
Mrs Wright in lime-green slacks
and mint-green blouse takes
hobbled steps neck stiff as any queen's:
arthritis and old age   Sacred
to ancient pharoahs the ibises
ignore her grunting thoughtfully
urnk urnk croo croo croo
no songbirds they but emblems for the eye . . .

To our dark left skiffs feather into mangrove
their cargo such stuff that dreams
are made on: temples and chariots
bought with hundred-dollar bills
Our cities decay like Karnak and
Dahshur shaken by violent children
while Mrs Wright in her tight slacks
minces along her husband polishing his
Chrysler LeBaron outside their barred
windows   They hate rap and Jap
Chicanos teachers even the white
ibises that soil their grass-colored stones . . .

O Florida our Flowerland we need to worship
something beyond ourselves to learn
something in detail to love something
alive not a flag or a car but something
that breathes maybe anything
that breathes like the ibises here on our lawn
(we know it works: Egyptians knelt in their
shadows thousands of years!)   But now

Mr Wright honks his horn and the ibises rise
See how they glide in diagonal lines:
a cuneiform code across our petrified sky
spelling a holy word we can no longer read . . .

In Memoriam

The day that James O Black
tiptoed over the tops
of the straightbacked

Sunday pews he was
wearing his dark-blue suit
and his brown catspaw shoes

Soldiers of Christ Arise
was rising from the choir
when James rose in the back

behind the Sunday hats
and mildly leapt toward the front
like a cat who had seen the light

Balancing on his soles
he stepped with winelit grace
arms flung out wide

his smile was sanctified
as he crossed the thirty rows
without breaking stride

The choir squealed to a stop
ushers paddled about
the flock fingered their hymnals

and didn't know what to think
while the minister improvised
on the evils of drink

But the children agreed that if
they could have a Sunday again
(a dubious blessing at best)

the one that they would choose
was the day that James O Black
  tiptoed over the backs of the marveling wooden pews

J J Nortle

J J Nortle waited each day
for the mail
for the acceptance of poems
he never wrote
and never sent
(he always meant to write
& send them) consequently
he was especially nervous
the chance being so small

He knew there was almost
no chance at all
but would wait perspiring
slightly an hour before
the postman came
and would run out
through snow and rain
(it was always the same:
through snow and rain)
to receive the usual prose
addressed to occupant
but each day he would burn
for the mail and run out
hoping for the word
on his poem to return

At last it came

The postman waltzed it right
to the door
whistling through sunshine as if
he had done it before

J J read: Congratulations
on your poem *The Lover*
which we will feature
on our Easter cover
Check to follow
                    Weeping
J J Nortle took the
letter to bed where they
found him two weeks later
the postman said

Japanese Soldier

. . . deep in a simmering jungle where
green light filters through vine and palm
an elderly soldier will not surrender

He hasn't heard of the peace or the bomb
the cold war or bloody korea
the german wall estonia vietnam

He holds in his cave no sony transistor
but there where he squats in swampy guam
waits each day for the boot of his emperor

to bless the shore with calm and victorious
step o beloved sun-king conqueror
Who is to call to him without qualm

Come out come out ? The law
stiff in his aging brain like a brazen charm
keeps him convinced his defiance has some

importance his country and home
are concerned and will always remember
the purity of his passion   Owning

nothing living on lizards shellfish coconut
water still he defends his farm
his fading wife and son near okayama

in darkness in tatters immortal in love on guam . . .

John Keyes & Freud

Professor Keyes doodled eyes
up & down his notebooks school books
diaries scratch pads even one in the mean
restroom of Big Dad's Pizza Palace:
big eyes bad eyes bloodshot brown
blueblackgreen: wherever John was
eyes were to be seen

And the professor wondered
What does it mean?

Are these wombs with pupils?
'I' eyes or cosmic eyes
negative I's or affirmative ayes?
Am I searching for a vision?
Afraid of going blind?   Are
they man-eyes or womanize
cruel I's or kind?

And back behind his brow
a thought squinted to get out:

John maybe you drew them
because you could
and continue because you can:
remember you once drew
a whole head of a man
but
it didn't look good

Kissing

I remember when we used to kiss
Your eyes closed for a moment then opened as if
in wonder at the world's sweet surprises of tongues of lips

We'd sit on the edge of the forbidden bed antic-
ipation bursting like cocaine   *Oyesyesyes*
I *remember* when we used to kiss!

Nothing's like touch like skin on skin
and every minute the young beginning to sip
in wonder at the world's sweet surprises of tongues of lips

of taste and smell: the rollercoaster dips
of the body's bends   And still through a myopic mist
I remember when we used to kiss

everywhere! lunatic lovebugs repetitive
as villanelles in your old jeep crying with bliss
and wonder at the world's sweet surprises of tongues of lips

We'd say pupils wide with excess *Do that!   Do this!*
What innocence!   What wickedness!
How I remember when we used to kiss
in wonder at the world's surprises: *Tongues!   And lips!*

Letting Go

after Dana Gioia

We think there's no heaven and no hell

just a panicked descent
into what's called darkness
but is worse than that:
grey silk between mirrors
each reflecting nothing but
mouse-grey silk forever
which is why we love the tug of water
friction of tree trunks
dry stones scraping our supple feet

No heaven no hell

So when Death's chalky finger screaks our way
how the heart skips
its fishy valves pumping toward
the finish line until the ribbon
breaks and we slide between
those empty stands of no resistance
spinning out of our corroded selves
memory leaking like acid
from a battery in hell . . .

but there *is* no hell

Already I'm letting go   What
happened to yesterday?   Where in heaven
are our children?   I forget our telephone
number and just this noon
drove the wrong way down Fourth Street
Or maybe Fifth   Soon they'll take my license
and lock me in a mouse-grey

humanitarian trap like the one in our attic
biting everything that moves

even your hand with its crumbs of love

M₃

Meaning (call it M_3) is the increasingly invisible
odorless tasteless element in our universe long ago
slipped by Someone's god into our water which if only we had
the proper instruments we'd recognize as H_2OM_3
But we who specialize in seeing trees instead of forests can
find in its place only particles of emptiness vibrating
randomly like the snowflakes in Greensboro during this Blizzard
of '96 for which we are as unprepared as Sodom or
Gomorrah were for flames

Of course we're as innocent and guilty as either of those doomed
cities without having had as much fun: our exercise and food
increasingly designed to extend our lives and make them not worth
living Winters *are* getting colder and soon by geologic
time the curled wave will freeze the stars wink shut the last love
        letter sent
All this is good   as the storm has shown us over and over: wheels
without friction spin uselessly digging existential ditches
heading nowhere at high speed   Clearly we should stay at home
        stock some
staples renew our vows

Without contraries there is no progression Blake proclaimed   That's why
I'm counting syllables here as a ground to grip: the miracle
of ordinary happiness demands connection lip to lip
hand on hand a boot biting into snow   It's the *recognition*
of connection (call *it* M_3 as well) that's become so hard: here
in Greensboro too far from you I know you've sent with deepest
        faith
your guardian spirit in whom I'm striving to believe and who
indeed seems to have brought me through to this snowed-in sunlit
        land of
dwindling milk and honey

Magnolia

Trees know nothing about personal fulfillment:
when our magnolia dances bright as a chorus
girl on opening day its sap doesn't get smug
but moves on to the next thing slipping its smooth leaves
like a card shark maybe or pushing a far branch
toward the beckoning sky: always something to do

Our particular tree is an ancient Bull Bay
Magnolia that will never reach its full glory
because it's in the shade of even taller oaks
It doesn't moan about lost potential or wish
it were on Wilson's lawn instead of ours under
full sun and with luck (when Mr. Wilson's sober)
judicious pruning some iron chelate in spring

No our old Bay hangs in there like a minor league
third baseman with aching knees working the pitcher
for a walk concentrating on the game itself
and out of the shade and acid soil it squeezes
yet one more blossom flooding the hot corner of
our yard with cream and honey: just doing its job

Making Love with the One

making love with the one
armed girl in the library
conference room one
reflects that everything
in one's life was leading

to this moment and in one

half hour everything
will be leading away
though why this should be
neither the librarian nor the one
armed girl is inclined to say

A Meditation on You and Wittgenstein

Wittgenstein never met you face to face
but fancied someone like you when he said
The world is everything that is the case

a maxim hard to fathom   Nevertheless
its rhythms tug like Ariadne's thread:
the world *is* everything that is the case

the world's *everything* that is the case
(you for example sleeping in my bed)
Although Wittgenstein never met you face to face

he guessed logic lies in poetry's embrace
and from the same dark labyrinth has fed
the world being everything that is the case:

for love or dreams of love curls at its base
and if you miss it your heart's bled and dead
I wish he could have met you face to face

An ounce of loneliness outweighs a pound of lace:
what strange equations winding through my head!
Poor Wittgenstein never met you face to face
The world is only everything: *that's* the case

Mulch

There where the punk stump marks
the end of our yard   we've strung
chickenwire around a six-by-six
plot of crabgrass   In theory
we apply a neat layer of leaves
a layer of leftovers like eggshells and coffee grounds
and then another layer of leaves
ad infinitum or *nauseam* whichever
comes first   In practice of course
we just toss in whatever's at hand:

sawdust and guacamole corncobs
and grass cuttings willy-nilly
in gross disorganization where
they decay and ooze together
like some vegetable Dorian Gray
until in spring and fall we spread it
below allamanda and oleander
camellia and azalea choking the weeds
holding in moisture making
spectacular over-achievers of them all

If only we could mulch our own mistakes
before they harden and stain
dropping the rinds of argument and affair
shells of dead dreams nasty shocks
skins of bad habits lumps of neglect
and sad pride into a pile
that bubbles and burns in the dark
until it's usable and by using
we'd learn for a change
and open and soar like hollyhocks in a country garden

Multiple Readings in National Poetry Month

We look out and see a clutch of drowning women
reaching for poems like branches dangling just over
their heads hoping to pull themselves to shore   A few
men slump there as well already sunk in whiskey
more addictive than poetry
For them an average ball game is livelier
than the average poem unless . . . maybe . . . *AND NOW
ENTERING THE GAME AT SMALL FORWARD:*
     WILLIE YEATS! . . .

Where was I? . . . I think the women are right: if food
and sex are all that matters a dog's life upbeat
and flatulent would be better than ours   But dogs
are neither disturbed nor soothed by verbal magic:
And the white breast of the dim sea
And all dishevelled wandering stars . . . Across our
audience hope and grace bloom like peonies
after summer rain heads nodding with intricate

incandescence our poem a twig a flimsy spray . . .
Still who can tell? The branch may not break but like a
fiberglass wand bearing far more than its own weight
pull us all together to a temporary
clearing the sky making both sense
and beauty the high-pitched stars singing their linked songs
the trees calling also   *We have meaning meaning:*
the animals staring with large reflective eyes

Nailbiters

How we long to love our parents
those cartoons of domesticity
whose foolish rages & incomprehensible
depressions made us what we are today:
Father why do I drink so much?
Mother why do I chew my nails?

Freud implied that biting fingernails
is self-mutilation from guilt our parents
laid on us for wetting the bed too much
failing Latin or getting lost on the City
subway when they took us out for a day
at the World's Fair   A lot of bull

of course but still it's a terrible
habit no matter how many denials
or lame excuses we invent   Each day
we pay homage in this way to parents'
power admitting our paucity
of inner resources by mouthing much-

soiled thumbs nipping as much
nail as is left like starved cannibals
forced to devour themselves with a ferocity
best used on neighbors   Father sometimes nailed
me with the back of his hand: it was apparent
he was really mad at the way his day

had gone or what Mother had done that day
but he couldn't hit a woman not much
anyway so I was elected   Parents
yearn to love their children with a noble
affection but it just slips aside hard to nail
down why exactly   The duplicity

of life stems from its seeming simplicity:
with the way that day follows day
in unbearably banal
ways until it's simply too much
and we have to scream and rebel
by misbehaving   children and parents

especially parents because how much longer
their daily disappointment! We all live to love burn
for reciprocity: *in absentia* we nibble our nails

Naked Poetry

Catholics have always known
nakedness embraces sacredness:
how the heart's mouth
yearns to strip
if only in a box or on a page
for strangers with downcast eyes

Words reined in too long
implode on liver and lung:
hermit crabs scraping
the veins' lanes
until they find a hole

to hunker in
Look at my hands
their ragged nails
I press them

together as if to pray:
here's the church here the steeple
Poets are

unhealthy people
whether sinful or too pure:

Writing is the only cure

No Circe

. . . we always forgive
the swinishness of the great
that trough of lust and betrayal:
Slaves to a cruel muse we say
blown by blind winds
cursed by holy thunder   Look
    what they've done for us:
    that poem that painting that
    exquisite purse . . .

. . . but I say Forgive
the sins of the ungreat
who have no Circe
no consolation
for the porcine pettiness
deep in our mean hearts
    And besides
    a lot of those so-called pearls
    are boring as pigshit . . .

Nor Iron Bars

All day we've been measuring bars
drilling them deep between window

and screen sweating and cursing
and skinning our knuckles pretending

their curlicues look continental:
but it's still prison and not

of flesh only   Even in sleep we see
the young boy on our stairs

> *his fear*
> *mirroring*
> *our fear*

and though we think we know
why he crouched at the end of a bad road

that began across oceans and decades
leading precisely to our shaded street

where twisted oaks hold witness
reason quails in confrontation: *angels alone*

that soar above enjoy such liberty
and now we have bars on our windows

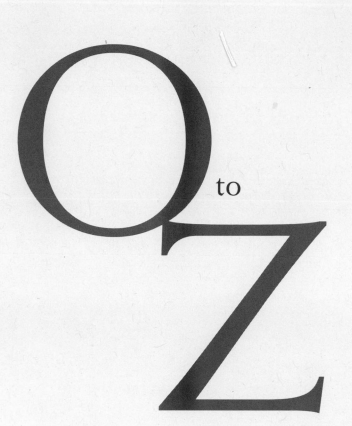

O'
to
Z

On the Road

America's cheerful in the morning: *Coffee*
coffee! Who wants coffee? chirp the fat ladies at
Wafflehouses across the land   The cooks' yellow
ambidextrous fingers flip the eggs and pancakes
and on all sides the men call *How far you goin'?*
Howfaryougoin'?

Only at night after not selling quite as much
as we hoped caffeine breaking down and running out
the spotted curtains not entirely closed the chained
tvs finally fast asleep the Camrys cool-
ing off squatting over crumbling macadam like
Japanese beetles

only then does silence surprise our ears like the
sweet birdsong we heard one time long ago calling
just to us: we ran through the street heart swelling with
wordless knowledge seeing for the first time the trees
around us the noble elms gorgeous and diseased
aching toward heaven

The Open

Watching Steffi beat Monica on t
v at Fat Jack's in Provincetown I was
seized with an urge as I sometimes am to
write a syllabic poem on the spot which
was none too clean and packed to the gills with
elbows and shrimp   Hey Sparky I yelled to
the bartender you got a pen?   Sure he
said knowing my propensities make it
ten syllables a line   Well why not I
said but on the other hand why?   Because
look this is the tenth game of the third set
Sparky said so I smoothed out the napkin
while the crowd screamed You can do it! and wrote
Watching Steffi beat Monica on t

Our Groundhog

squats like a sack of potatoes
in a field of alfalfa
his behind wobbling
as he slips into his lair
a spy in a phone booth
furtive and furry

or like an artist solitary
and out of shape stubbornly
devouring his surroundings
old eyes acquainted
with nature's betrayal
and delayed gratification

or like the rest of us his voice
a silly whistle in the dark
guarding his nest so his pups
born naked and blind
will open their eyes to summer
rolling in clover

Pensacola

Let's make the assumption that we're all friends
not because it's true but because it's more
interesting   Who else cares if I
look from my window on a flight from Pensacola

and see the morning moon minted like a dime
a young sun warming the leaky mattress
of clouds?   Sleepless I've been away too long
the plane is cold my seat malicious

and inflexible   In nasal monotone
the stewardess demonstrates devices
to save us if the plane disintegrates
against a mountain   I take deep breaths

to calm myself look for the exit   *In case
of dismemberment*   she sings   *do not
inflate the flotation cushion*   My world
is teetering in the balance not

in these icy skies but on the ground
where someone's waiting   I notice on the wing
four wires sticking out and wonder
about the plane's design: everything

seems random out of order even
this earth below not perfectly round
but flattened at the poles bulging and dented
I wanted to write this in the first person jugular

confessing weaknesses and sins while isolated
in purer air like a microbe in God's lung
but get distracted by multiple
stimuli and the fear that someone

might *not* be waiting after all
Bright pools dot the neighborhoods
below like celestial inkwells   I can't blame her
I never wrote but have always hoped

for better than I deserve
The earth rotates from West to East
objects in the mirror are closer
than they appear we read from left

to right   her eyes are manzanilla
I have a prolapsed mitral valve
so my heart murmurs her name:
these are the facts   But facts can't save

love or poetry only music can
speaking broadly   It's funny
the way art works if this is art:
through pretending it can become

real a kind of temporary fact
hanging in the air between us
like a song that brings tears
and smiles to our eyes simultaneously

linking our disparate isolate years
because I know as we near the end
here I've told you a few secrets
and that does make us sort of friends

though I still can't identify the nearest exit

Philosophy in Billy's Bar

Language is the whorehouse of the imagination   *I say*
to Billy who looks doubtful   one eye stuck on the
Bucs' game *Y'want the mega-pepperoni?*   he asks *What*
noodles!   The latter I gather refers to the Bucs so I
nod and nudge my glass toward him for another belt
of RedWolf Outside the heat could bend a nickel and
drivers weep in stalled clusters as freon leaks from
their laboring a/c's   Everything's connected and runs
on friction they say: one totally perfect object would
shut down the world   which makes me a tiny bit
nervous about this very poem which is humming
along like a Beamer up to now though it has perhaps
one too many *which's*   so I decide to leave them in
and save us all as Billy returns lugging four beers his
personal contribution to the liquidation of the human
spirit

Pickpockets

To them everything feels heavy
resistant   billfolds and watches
dragging like barnacled anchors
against the tips of their fingers
Pallid and pudgy as squid they
labor long hours submerged in
stygian subways pressed belly
and butt to cheap polyester
eyes bulging with disappointment
By now they thought they'd be Bible

salesmen breathing erotic old
stories to bored housewives or watch
repairmen with their own shops on
Ocean Avenue nine to five
then home to Susie Salvaggio
whose unpadded bra they unhooked
with one hand in the Nurse's Rest
Room at the Junior Prom   Instead
they cruise their beats in rumpled suits
that are hard to remember their

boneless hands nosing like carp through
crusted doubloons   Sleeping poorly
they dream of open spaces where
gravity's void and wallets float
like lilies on prodigal air
the diaphanous dresses of
expensive women rising as
the seven veils of Salomé
must have hovered O *weightless* in
the guilty Galilean night

Possibility

When I dove into the lake at midnight searching
for your glasses the moonlight shriveling at my
back like icicles at noon I pushed down and down
hands fanning through reeds and weeds and startled sunfish
looking for love more than anything and thinking
or feeling rather that everything's limitless
the lake the evening the moon and most of all you:

even your glasses (all you wore forgotten on
that forbidden swim) so rich in complexity
their history could fill volumes and still not touch
the artistry of curve above your ear precise
pressure holding them in place so you couldn't tell
they were on but only felt their absence coming
up fast to breathe after our underwater kiss

panic rushing in with the stars and the sweet night
air and thoughts of explanations to your parents:
*It was a robber sir snatched them right off her while
we watched the movie* What movie? Any movie
We knew we wouldn't be good at this so I said
Don't cry I'll find them took the deepest breath of my
life and plunged like a white lance toward the waiting grail

You can do anything you want to me you'd said
and I a high school boy who knew nothing about
anything grew dizzy from possibility
which is always there like gravity even though
the odds are bad: and though they slam the bars on us
over and over *it's still there* trembling in the
dark like glasses on the bottom of Rainbow Lake

The Professor and the Librarian

Here in the college collecting dust
  books and professors huddle together
Professor Crookshank studying lust
  talks with Miss Bailey about the weather

Is that a cirrus cloud you think?
  Clouds is clouds Miss Bailey said
Look at that one tinged with pink!
  Balls on pink she gaily said

Your eyes quoth he *are nothing like*
  the sun   Some think they're bright enough
the nymph replied   He said *Your thighs*
  are marbled pillars   She said Can that stuff

Professor Crookshank courted her
  through several centuries of lyric verse
He was the stricken cavalier
  besprent by Aphrodite's curse

He wrote a sonnet to her breasts
  an ode upon her tiny shoe
She wrote a memo to attest
  that Herrick's poems were overdue

His mind was blind and couldn't see
  the way to leave her or detest her
compiled a bibliography
  of love throughout the fall semester

And when Miss Bailey turned him down
  he wept real tears upon real rocks
and sang a melancholy song
  to bored imaginary flocks

The Queen Ant's Love Song

for Caitlin

I didn't know I was a queen   I just felt BIG
Right from the beginning I blew up a black blimp
the others scurrying around busybusy
They wouldn't let me feed myself and pretty soon
I couldn't: I just lay there like a sock waiting
watching my pale wings grow two veined enormous kites
Terrific   I'll never *get off the ground* I thought
Who designed this mishmash that's what I want to know
There were others with wings smaller but I liked them:
one in particular his eyes brighter somehow
his shell clean and shiny as a new toy   He was
a show-off too prancing around my fat body
licking it sometimes I would have stroked his head if
I could move fast enough which I damn well couldn't

So I lay there thinking *Is this it?* What am I
supposed to do? The day I found out I woke up
and the nest was alive even I was shaking
The little ones   females who fed me and cleaned me
were using their tiny heads to push me out of
the nest a regular barn-raising spectacle

The winged males came with me and my body said *Choose*
and my body said *Fly* I was on the ground strain-
ing   males buzzing above kamikaze pilots
around a hurt bomber and I looked for the one
I liked and saw him high so I pulled myself up
on a plant up and up and out on a broad leaf
until I was near him and spread out my wings like
SAILS   and then I jumped in the air *And he was there*

Revelation

. . . in the end Keats's stone will go
when mountains crack asunder
and salt stain Michelangelo
and drown the bird of wonder
The earth will pitch to black of night
to prove the scientists are right:
a scientific meteorite
will bury science under

Exploding planets are the sound
of God's terrific laughter
and chips of moon come scaling down
from heaven's cosmic rafter
We know as suns descend like Mars
to melt the metal motor cars
angels existed before the stars
but what comes twinkling after? . . .

Seven & Seven

Looking back at it now he
can see what a fool he was
but life's not a damn exam

and if being a dunce and
disgrace has dragged him to where
he kneels in this sweltering

sagging house with the shutters
hanging like drunks from a frayed
merry-go-round a pen or

a drink in his hand and her
reading a book while the dogs
circle outside maniacs

running the land no matter
which way we vote he can say
at least we tried and this the

road we took: *twisting below*
the oaks the vines sucking their
trunks where unearthly shadows
mix with the smell of salt and
decay and the swollen threat
of rain warps the cypress boards
and softens the porous ground
until the house tilts like a
monk tipsy beside a stream
that murmurs the drunkard's dream:

Everything can be fixed O
Lord anything can be fixed

She, Being an Artist

She being an artist understood
delayed gratification her touch
and tongue lingering perhaps an inch
•from driving them crazy   Womanhood

was a state she elected to study
resolving at an early age
to polish her given gifts uncaging
the innate forces of her body

the way Picasso and Dickinson
let the wind howl through their fingers
to bend the world   There was nothing
she didn't try or try again

overcoming the equivalent
of writer's block by sheer desire
till she and her partners were on fire
at exactly the intensity she meant

She *knew* she was an artist: it
was her way of publishing giving more
pleasure than any passionate score
boldfaced page rounded stone stiff

canvas until she became a heroic
endowment all by herself granting
her lucky applicants the best gift
in the world: their own dreams at work

and she funded both women and men
not without discrimination but
in abandoned abundance so that
eventually her largesse extended

across state lines in fact
across any line you or I can imagine
a lagoon of honey bubbling
over its bed sweetening every pebble in its path

Short Meditation on Long-Suffering Poets

Although they say that suffering helps us write
tears have nothing to do with making poems:
I know a man who rocks and moans all night
and every line he cries lies dry as bone
Teardrop and *blood-drop* are only words
and though one write like Faust in reddest ink
unsealing veins of salt that bite and burn
it's vowels and consonants not blood we drink

The nightingale's a feather of a bird:
nature's breath can knock it head to tail
A poet should be tougher   Some have heard
the mockingbird scaling like a nightingale
I know a woman hasn't wept for years:
and every syllable she writes sheds tears

Sort of a Sonnet

Say what you mean! he says *Be clear for once*
in your life Outside she sees young men
bending out of cars combing their hair
in the light rain and thinks or
almost thinks . . . *in this shadow*
of a raindrop across the damask cloth
light gathers . . . in some complicated manner
but it's there . . .
               As she studies his face
in the mottled window a Rabbit with its lights on
drives through his eyes *I can't say this*
she almost thinks again and says *I'll try*
while black leaves turn silver in the wind
and acorns rattle the slanted roof
with a noise as clear and mean as simple truth

The Teacher

for Robert Detweiler, on his retirement

If laughter's the brightest blade on the Lord's
lawn He grafted on you His broad green thumb:
when lines furrow by your eyes we see jokes
building like spring rain and your delight in
them doubles our fun

What do we want from our friends if not a
lifting once in a while of the world's weight?
I see you hunched at your desk eyes inches
from a book light beams slanted with dust mim-
icking galaxies:

motes of gold with their satellites circling
the sun   Beauty's everywhere miracles
daily and something lit the world like a
wick: you were glad to call it God   *What we
need's not judgment but*

love   you'd tell us *which doesn't mean that Dean
So&so isn't full of shit*   Around
the country now students at their daily
tasks stop every once in a while and smile
at some memory

of you slouched by the board turning toward them
to ask *OK who watched* Star Trek *last night?*
beginning the dialogue: remembering
not only how you were funny but how
you made them realize

*Though the big things happen outside of books
books too are vital: our best words & thoughts
pooling on paper oases in a
desert of dying verbs granting our parched
selves this rare chance:*   Drink

75

Les Temps Modernes

At Buddha's birth
the skies trembled and roared
but when I was born
only my mother yelled crying
What's going on anyway?

When Jesus broke bread it multiplied
feeding the multitudes
but my Wonder Bread
is already sliced
my kids scarf it down at one sitting

and when Bodhidharma buried his eyelids
tea plants grew
but when I planted my tongue
the grass died and the ground cracked dry
That's no way to start a religion

Tough Professor Sonnet

Crazy! He flunked the lazy wafflers right
and left while all his colleagues let them slide
on by like sheep through dip   At any rate
both high- and single-handedly he slowed
their march toward mediocrity that root
rot of our time (he said) where we've mislaid
the standards we used to know by rote:
Democracy's a sloppy-minded slut

Of course they hated him   They squealed like pigs
beneath the knife when he returned a paper
bright with blood   But because they were square pugs
who paid tuition they paid the piper
too and he was fired   In time the pegs
grew fat in their round holes: he died a pauper

The Uniform

He has always suspected uniformed
people: even these Cub Scouts' uninformed
innocence seems wrong like a unicorn
with an erection Their slight cuneiform
figures scrawl across the church gymnasium
floor some ancient warning in Sumerian
or Suburban a cryptic multiform
message on adolescent onionskin
that he the proud father must decipher
Something to do with the lack of laughter:
his bright bubbly boy goes dry right after
he puts one on Like his own pin-striped suit
maybe   it means business Something to do
with that shadow crisscrossing the rafter

Vincent

One time Vincent snapped Melinda's arm
like a chopstick though really
she broke it herself trying to pull out
of his fat beige fingers wrapped
almost double around her skinny wrist

We were kids and we poked and tortured
Vincent because he was fat slow and different
towering over us his face from another planet
green and slack his talk a whine
we couldn't translate Our parents told us

Let him alone! And I sometimes think
if we had only obeyed them Melinda and I
might have been happy I suppose even
children should pay for their sins *but Vincent*
we're sorry please forgive us Her arm is fine

The Waltz

The Downtown Coliseum
   has ducked the wrecker's ball
   by the narrowest of votes

though we're warned it's bound to go
   in the next electric storm
   or a gale from off the coast

so our dances here are numbered
   and every Friday night
   fewer of us gather

beneath the sagging roof
   with its fake starlight
   in front of Mannie's band

which is also getting smaller
   Still we rise from our frayed booth
   holding each other's hand

as if one of us might fall:
   May I have another dance?
   And we step off once again

circling through a waltz
   on knees too stiff to bend
   My arthritic fingers play

slow imaginary notes
   across the back they know so well
   while the music seems to say

with the pink zinfandel
   Not all love is lost
   nor all consolations false

We used to bet a dime
   on who would tire more
   O we were dancing fools!

So we turn one last time
   more or less in tune
   across the pockmarked floor:

Scarecrows on the moon

The Wave

I was at the ninth line of my final poem the one
about 'the liquid / twittering of the swallows' when
it started: in the cheap seats Bukowski and Hollo
high-fived and flung their wine-stained shirts to the feminists

in the seventh row   Romantics with rosy lips made
swallow imitations modernists hid their eyes so
they could concentrate purely & the post-moderns stuffed
their ears so the words wouldn't confuse them   The critics

decided to be generous relaxing their hunched
shoulders in the sun   Ginsberg rang his little bells Bly
was hugging uncertain young men in fatherly ways
when the New Formalists loosened their ties and stood up

So they *all* stood up section after section throwing
their cramped arms in the air a wheatfield of poets on
a free afternoon baseball on strike the NEA
nowhere to be seen O and didn't we have a time!

No fans are crazy like mad-dog poetry fans: *One
more line!* they chanted *One . . . more . . . line!* I hesitated
only a moment and then wild with love for all of
us I threw the whole damn book into the ink-stained stands

The Witness

Like an aging eagle in its cage
he has outlived his gestures
the noble generosity the slow wink
that showed he saw right through us
and didn't disapprove   He has gone
querulous and mean who once bowled
through the cold sky over Cave Mountain
toward Catskill Creek squirming far below

What can he do but feed on memory
gold-flecked eyes trained inward on
the time he wheeled in amorous circles
above river and wreck our cries a ratlike squeak
as he patrolled the skies like God's
own hostile witness: a dark diminishing speck . . .

The Examiner's Death

Her life was blameless blameless
so when the Drivers License Examiner died
she went straight to the Vestibule of Heaven
It was crowded but after two centuries
she reached the desk   'Take a number'
said St. Christopher   'We'll call you'

'Two centuries and you'll call me?' she said

'You should've made an appointment' the saint mumbled
rubbing his halo like a hubcap

'How do you do that?'

'Not my department' he said   'Have a seat'

The Drivers' License Examiner could hear
choirs singing and the still hum of suns
buzzing like mopeds through the empyrean
This is timelessness   she thought   *There is
no time*   Shadows pooled and diminished
diminished and pooled forests rose and tumbled
between sheets of ice   In her dreams
her husband laughed his little
cough of a laugh

When her number was called
the man at the desk looked like God
eyes dark as inkpads

'Do you have your Death Certificate?' he asked

'How could I?   I was dead when they issued it!'

'Keep your voice down' said God pursing his lips
'We've got a problem'

The Young Poet Speaks

I straddle the bucking horse of poetry
waving high my heart
to the oblivious crowd craning
the other way to see
a donkey ridden by a naked tart
An old man shakes a grin at me
and yells 'Words ain't worth a fart!'
I smile:
>   *Each poem will be*
> *a dagger nailing to their breasts*
> *the resolution they will need*
> *to be their best*

His Teacher's Reply

This may be so   Try not to bleed
too much   Bother the rich   Try
to enjoy the rest

Zinc Fingers

Though scientists inform us that criminals
have insufficient zinc I've always believed
it's insufficient gold and silver that gets
them going   The man who slipped his hand into
my front pocket on the jammed Paris *Métro*
wasn't trying to make friends   His overcoat
smelled greasy and it was unpleasant holding
hands above my wallet pressed in on all sides
like stacked baguettes   There was no way to move or
take a swing   Still some action on my part seemed
to be called for: we stood nose to nose   I tried
to look in his eyes but he stared at my chin
shy on our first date so after a while as
we rattled along toward the Champs-Élysées

I lost concentration and began to think

of our scholarly daughter working at Yale
on a project called Zinc Fingers scanning a
protein with pseudopods each with a trace of
zinc that latch on to our DNA and help
determine what we become   This brought me back
to *mon ami* the pickpocket: I wondered
how he chose his hard line of work and if as
a boy he was good at cards for example
or sewing and for that matter what choice did
I have either so when we reached our stop and
he looked up from my chin at last I smiled at
him and his eyes flashed in fear or surprise and
I called *It's OK* as he scuttled away
Tout va bien! though I held tight to my wallet

Acknowledgments

Grateful acknowledgment is made to the following publications, in which most of the poems in this collection first appeared: *5 AM* ("Kissing," "Philosophy in Billy's Bar," "The Waltz"); *9 MM: Poets Respond to Violence in America* ("Vincent"); *America* ("Zinc Fingers"); *American Poetry Monthly* ("Possibility"); *Atlanta Review* ("History"); *Caprice* ("Our Groundhog"); *Carolina Quarterly* ("Fortunato Pietro," "The Humane Trap," "Seven & Seven"); *Christian Century* ("Les Temps Modernes"); *Eckerd College Review* ("A Handheld Camera Visits Billy's Bar at Happy Hour"); *Epos* ("Coal"); *Florida Quarterly* ("The Professor and the Librarian"); *The Formalist* ("Home on Cape Cod," "The Tough Professor Sonnet," "The Witness"); *Georgia Review* ("Assisted Living," "Naked Poetry," "She, Being an Artist"); *Greensboro Review* ("The Brain"); *Gulf Stream Magazine* ("Mulch"); *Kalliope* ("The Housekeeper in London," "Multiple Readings in National Poetry Month"); *Konglomerati* ("Coffee"); *The Laurel Review* ("A Hot Day in June"); *Light Year '87* ("The Examiner's Death"); *Many Mountains Moving* ("Japanese Soldier"); *Michigan Quarterly Review* ("Revelation"); *motive* ("J J Nortle"); *New CollAge Magazine* ("Making Love with the One"); *New Letters* ("The Cliff at Gorge de l'Areuse," "Ibises"); *New Republic* ("Each Morning"); *Nit&Wit* ("Driving Through a Storm near Boothbay Harbor"); *Poet Lore* ("Grandfather at the Pool," "The Plains of Mars"); *Poetry* ("Apples," "M_3"); *Poetry International* ("On the Road"); *Poetry Venture* ("Circe"); *Press* ("In Memoriam"); *Red Mud Review* ("Certitude"); *River City* ("Pensacola"); *Scholia Satyrica* ("Election"); *Shenandoah* ("Pickpockets"); *Smashing Icons* ("No Circe"); *State Street Review* ("Absence," "Sort of a Sonnet"); *Stringtown* ("Nailbiters," "Nor Iron Bars"); *Tampa Review* ("Arthritis in St. Petersburg," "Finches on Aycock Street," "A Meditation on You and Wittgenstein," "The Queen Ant's Love Song"); *Tar River Poetry* ("Short Meditation on Long-Suffering Poets"); *Tennessee Quarterly* ("The Wave"); *To Honor a Teacher* ("The Teacher"); *Zone 3* ("Francis," "Letting Go," "Magnolia," "The Open").

Many thanks also to the University of North Carolina at Greensboro, the Writer's Voice Project in Tampa, Eckerd College in St. Petersburg, and the Château de Lavigny in Switzerland for appointing me writer-in-residence at various times, during which most of these poems were written.

And thanks to Arthur Skinner of Eckerd College for making the slides of the artwork from which the cover was made.